FÀILTE MALAWI

A global citizenship resource for primary schools

INTRODUCTION

This resource pack has been written in recognition of the number of schools in Scotland which have a connection with, or interest in, Malawi. It is not designed to give you lots of information about Malawi, (although we have provided some background material and useful websites) rather to use Malawi as a context for learning about rights, exploring Global Citizenship and to challenge perceptions and stereotypes of the world beyond the everyday experience of most pupils and teachers in Scotland.

This booklet contains a selection of examples from the CD ROM, to give you a flavour of the whole resource without having to access a computer. Although a few of these examples do require support material, you can find them on the CD ROM as well as the image galleries.

The resource has been designed to support the implementation of *Curriculum for Excellence*, and exemplify its principles and aims. Some activities have been designed specifically for level 1 or 2 and these are clearly indicated. Otherwise the activities can readily be differentiated for use at either level.

The reflection and evaluation sections in each activity support formative assessment and ongoing monitoring of pupils learning. Additional summative assessment opportunities have been highlighted within activities.

Activities suitable for Enterprise have also been highlighted. In addition, there are a number of activities which would be suitable to carry out with partner schools in Malawi and support the development of shared curriculum projects.

How to use this resource

We recommend that you start with some of the activities in the Core Activities section as this will enable you to establish a baseline from which you can evaluate pupils learning. This also includes core rights activities which should be completed before looking at further rights activities.

Each of the four themed sections contains Key Activities, Rights Activities and Topic Activities which enable you to build a programme of work for your pupils which delivers your priorities. You might take a rights approach, a topic approach or focus on Malawi. Topic activities can also be used to provide a Global Citizenship element to ongoing classroom work.

Literacy, numeracy and health and wellbeing activities have been built in across the resource and highlighted in the overview grid.

CONTENTS

Overview 2-3
Images of Malawi 4
Core activities 6
Rights activities 8
Homes 12
Toys 18
Food & farming 24
Water 30

CD ROM – *see inside back cover*

OVERVIEW

Core activities are about exploring our own attitudes and values. They relate mainly to images and perceptions and it is strongly recommended that these activities are carried out before any others in this resource. The activities also include baseline for assessing change in attitudes and thinking.

Key activities provide an introduction to the topic and encourage pupils to examine their initial thoughts and think about what they will learn and why.

The Rights activities can be used on their own to develop this area of work as a standalone unit.

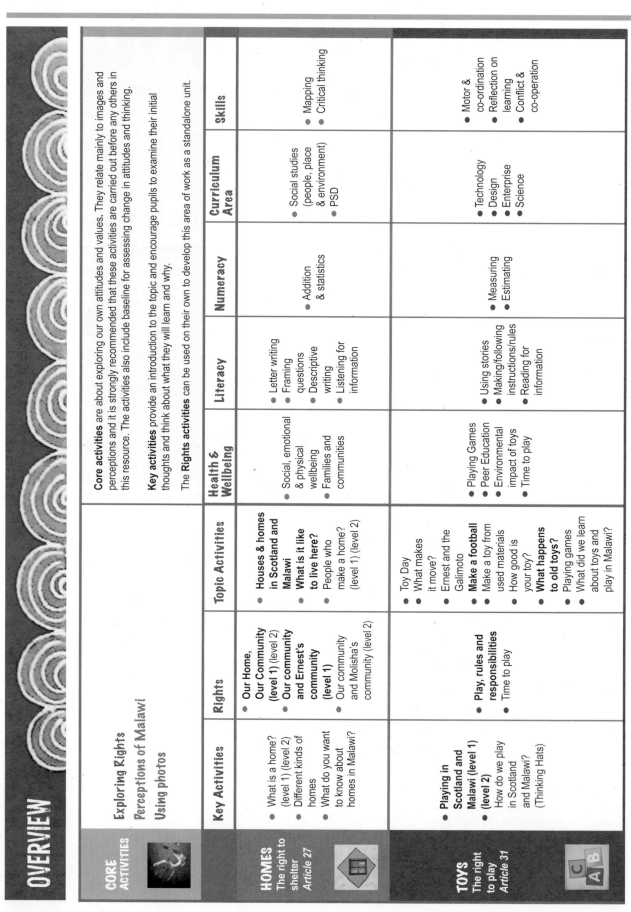

	Key Activities	Rights	Topic Activities	Health & Wellbeing	Literacy	Numeracy	Curriculum Area	Skills
CORE ACTIVITIES	Exploring Rights *Perceptions of Malawi* Using photos							
HOMES The right to shelter *Article 27*	• What is a home? (level 1) (level 2) • Different kinds of homes • What do you want to know about homes in Malawi?	• **Our Home, Our Community (level 1) (level 2)** • **Our community and Ernest's community (level 1)** • Our community and Molisha's community (level 2)	• **Houses & homes in Scotland and Malawi** • **What is it like to live here?** • People who make a home? (level 1) (level 2)	• Social, emotional & physical wellbeing • Families and communities	• Letter writing • Framing questions • Descriptive writing • Listening for information	• Addition & statistics	• Social studies (people, place & environment) • PSD	• Mapping • Critical thinking
TOYS The right to play *Article 31*	• **Playing in Scotland and Malawi (level 1)** • **(level 2)** • How do we play in Scotland and Malawi? (Thinking Hats)	• **Play, rules and responsibilities** • Time to play	• Toy Day • What makes it move? • Ernest and the Galimoto • **Make a football** • Make a toy from used materials • How good is your toy? • **What happens to old toys?** • Playing games • What did we learn about toys and play in Malawi?	• Playing Games • Peer Education • Environmental impact of toys • Time to play	• Using stories • Making/following instructions/rules • Reading for information	• Measuring • Estimating	• Technology • Design • Enterprise • Science	• Motor & co-ordination • Reflection on learning • Conflict & co-operation

Text in **BOLD** indicates content is shown in the this booklet. All content is on CD ROM.

	Key Activities	Rights	Topic Activities	Health & Wellbeing	Literacy	Numeracy	Curriculum Area	Skills
WATER The right to clean water *Article 27*	• Wonderful water! • **Fair use of water (level 2)**	• The water supply • **What happens if the water is cut off?**	• **Water and the daily routine** • Recording water use in Scotland • **Water usage in Malawi** • Too little or too much • Climate change mystery (level 2) • Climate change in Malawi (level 2)	• Physical health • Hygiene • Environment	• Listening & talking • Discussion for consensus • Listening for information • Writing summarising facts	• Measuring volume • Measuring time & distance • Estimating • 4 number processes • Collection, recording & presentation of data	• Science • People, place and environment • RME	• Actions & consequences • Problem solving • Research & investigation • Group working • Presentation
FOOD & FARMING The right to nutritious food *Article 27*	• What is a farm? (level 1) • **What do you know about farming? (level 2)** • What does a farmer do?	• How healthy is our diet? • Nutritious healthy food for all • Sugar trade game • Fair trade – take action!	• Where does our breakfast come from? • **What do we want from our food?** • On my farm • Farming vocabulary • Local farm study • **Cash crops or subsistence farming (level 2)?** • **Subsistence farming in Malawi (level 2)** • Sugar farming in Malawi (level 2) • How sugar is processed (level 2)	• Physical health • Healthy eating • Environment	• Listening & talking • Listening for instruction • Building vocabulary: dictionaries/ glossaries • Reading for information • Reading for understanding • Arguing effectively	• Graphs • Numbers	• Expressive arts (role play) • RME • Science (food technology) • People, place and environment	• Problem solving • Negotiating • Group co-operation • Research & investigation

Text in **BOLD** indicates content is shown in the this booklet. All content is on CD ROM.

IMAGES OF MALAWI

Many of the activities in this resource make use of photos and you will find a bank of images on the CD ROM. We have tried to avoid stereotypical images of poverty and hope these photos will encourage empathy and a sense of commonality with children in Malawi. They are used in the pack to explore attitudes and values as well as a tool for critical thinking. Many of the activities also use photos of Scotland so that pupils can reflect on the similarities and differences between their lives and the lives of Malawian children. We have included some images from Scotland and suggest that pupils and teachers create their own photo sets to use with the topics.

Maize is a staple crop in Malawi and used to make porridge or nsima. Sometimes it is taken to a mill for grinding, or sometimes women pound it by hand.

90% of the population in Malawi live in rural areas and many are subsistence farmers. Much of the labour on the land is done by hand or using traditional farming methods.

Women pounding maize.

Maize.

Women using hoes to prepare the soil for planting maize.

Most villages and towns will have a market place. Subsistence farmers will often sell surplus produce at the market.

The larger towns and cities have shops selling a wide range of goods.

Selling tomatoes at a local market.

Inside a supermarket in Lilongwe.

A typical shop.

As in Scotland, there is a wide variety of house types in Malawi including traditional rural houses built from mud with thatched roofs and modern homes which look similar to ours. More photos of houses can be found on page 13.

A modern urban house.

A traditional rural home.

Children in Malawi are more likely to have toys they have made themselves than shop bought ones. Ball games, especially football and netball are very popular. Sometimes children will use balls they have made with plastic bags. More photos of toys and play can be found on page 20.

Boys playing with the toy cars they have made.

Playing with a doll.

Water is collected in a variety of ways in Malawi. In rural areas women and children will often have to pump water from a communal pump and carry it back in buckets to their houses. Towns may have a water kiosk where water can be bought and collected. In cities some people will have water piped into their houses.

Carrying water home.

Collecting water from a kiosk. (Wateraid)

Pumping water by hand.

Bath time.

Having a drink.

Pulling up water from a well.

CORE ACTIVITIES

This exercise has been designed as a baseline to measure pupils' knowledge, attitudes and perceptions of Malawi prior to teaching and learning. The activity should be repeated after the pupils have covered a programme of work.

Aims

- To find out what the pupils think and know about Malawi

What you need

- Large blank sheet of paper for each group or student
- Recording template (CD ROM)

What to do

Brainstorm all the countries the pupils know in Africa and locate them on a map. Include Malawi!
Ask pupils 'What would you see in Malawi?' or 'What do you know about Malawi?'
Ask them to write or draw their ideas onto the large sheet of paper. This can be done individually or in groups. Teachers can label drawings, if necessary for clarification.
Record comments made and explanations where possible.

Teacher prompts

Are there any people?
What would they be doing?
What would they look like?
Are there any buildings?
What would they look like?
What would you see growing?

How to evaluate the baseline

The recording sheet is used to analyse and interpret the results of the activity:
- Classify the comments under the headings shown on the recording template. If there are multiples of the same comment, count each separately
- Calculate the percentage of the total comments in each category

Look for:
- The extent to which pupils show an awareness of diversity within and across a range of aspects of life, for example, between urban and rural, rich and poor, traditional and contemporary

How do you know if your teaching has been effective?
- When you repeat the activity you are looking for a more balanced range of responses across the categories and within each category, reflecting an increased awareness of the locality

N.B. This activity can be used to gauge pupils' knowledge and attitudes as their school embarks on a partnership with a school in another country. Repeats of the exercise can indicate the impact the partnership has had on learning and perceptions.

This activity has been adapted from How do we know it's working? - a toolkit for measuring attitudinal change in global citizenship from early years to KS5 RISC.

Using photographs

Photographs are a very valuable and flexible resource. They play an important part in forming our attitudes about other people and places. While they can help us make sense of the wider world they can also reinforce negative assumptions and stereotypes. The activities below introduce students to images of Malawi and also encourage them to begin to look critically at photographs. You will find more photo activities on the CD ROM which you could use to adapt or refocus the activities here.

Aims

• To introduce pupils to images of Malawi
• To encourage pupils to look closely at images and begin to question what they see

What you need

• A selection of photos of Malawi
• Flip chart or sugar paper

What to do (1)

Display the set of Malawi photos around the room. Ask the pupils to look at all the photographs and stand beside the one they like best. How does it compare with their initial ideas about Malawi? Pupils discuss in groups and feedback 3 points to the class.

What to do (2)

Organise pupils in groups and ask them to stick their photo into the middle of the sheet of paper. Groups should write down all the questions they have about the photograph on the paper around the photograph. Encourage them to think critically about the image and about what they would like to find out. Groups can then 'carousel' around the photos adding questions to the sheet. Use the evaluation and reflection points to hold a plenary. This activity can be used by the pupils to build an enquiry framework to structure their work on Malawi. See CD ROM for further ideas.

Teacher prompts

What can you see in the photo?
What are they doing?
What would you like to know about them/ask them?
How do you think these people feel: happy, tired, content, worried, etc?

Reflection and evaluation

How did the photos compare with your ideas/ brainstorm / picture map of Malawi? Was there anything in the photos which surprised you? If so what? Can a set of photos give you a true sense of a place? What photos could we use to give a 'true sense' of Scotland? What are some of the things to think about when using photos? What did you find out about Malawi from the photos?

Aims

- To introduce the concepts of needs and wants
- To introduce the idea of Children's Rights

What you need

- Pictures or objects which represent the following needs and wants: family, home (shelter), clean water (bottle), food item, play, sweets, TV, school (education), hospital (medical care), holiday, mobile phone, fashionable clothes.

What to do

Tell the pupils they are going to move to a new planet in space. They need to think about what they will need there to begin their new life. They need to create a place where children can live and grow up well. Show the pupils the objects and pictures representing needs and wants. You might need to explain what some of the objects / pictures represent.
Discuss each object in turn and think about what it stands for. Would they need it in their new world? Is it important for children?

The class vote to decide if they will take it to their new planet or not. During the discussion try and elicit the terms 'needs' and 'wants'. Divide the items into 'needs' and 'wants'. Discuss whether all children in Scotland and Malawi have their 'needs' and 'wants' met. Explain that these 'needs' are called 'rights'.

Teacher prompts

Do you all have these things (needs items)?
Should all children have these things?
Do you think all children in Scotland / Malawi have these things?

Reflection and evaluation

Thinking about Rights in Scotland and Malawi (Level 1)
on the CD ROM follows on from this and looks at children's rights in more detail.

CHILDREN'S RIGHTS

Aims
• To develop an understanding of what a 'right' is
• To find out how we are supported to claim our rights
• To be aware that rights bring responsibilities

What you need
• Sets of rights cards cut up for each group
• Set of scenario cards for each group

What to do (1)
Give each group a selection of rights. Explain that the rights can be put into 3 categories: self, services and protection. Ask the groups to divide their cards into the 3 groups.
OR
Give each group a selection of rights cards. Ask them
to rank the rights in order of importance.
Discuss with the groups how they made their selections using the teacher prompts.
Explain that while we all have rights, our rights can also affect others. We
must also think about our responsibility to ensure the rights of others are met.
Rights can be supported by us, by our families and by our communities.

What to do (2)
Give each group a set of scenario cards. Ask them to discuss which rights are highlighted in the scenario, how the rights could be supported and if there is anything they can do to ensure that rights of others are supported. Each group should feed back to the class.

Teacher prompts
Was it difficult to group some of the rights?
Which ones and why?
Are there some rights which are more important than others?
These are a selection of rights. Can you think of any others which you think are important?

Reflection and evaluation
Summarise what we mean by needs, wants, rights and responsibilities. Are these rights available to all children in their communities / Scotland / Malawi? How can we ensure others get their rights?

Every child has the right to life.

Every child has the right to a name and a nationality.

Every child has the right to be with their family or with those who will care for them best.

Every child has the right to enough food and clean water.

Every child has the right to an adequate standard of living.

Every child has the right to health care.

Every child with a disability has the right to special care and support.

Every child has the right to relax and play.

Every child has the right to privacy.

Every child has the right to education.

Every child has the right to be kept safe and not to be hurt or neglected.

No child should be used as cheap labour or as a soldier.

Children who break the law should not be treated cruelly.

Every child has the right to speak their own language and practise their own religion.

Every child has the right to say what they think and be heard.

Every child has the right to meet their friends and join groups.

CHILDREN'S RIGHTS

1. Jane lives with her Mum who is in a wheel chair. Jane often has to stay at home to help look after her as she can't manage on her own.

2. Iris was doing well at school and wanted to become a doctor. However, since her father left to find work in the city she has to stay at home and help with work on the farm.

3. Soloman lives in a village with his parents and 2 brothers and sister. They didn't have any mosquito nets and his baby sister got sick with malaria. They had to take her to the hospital 5 miles away. By the time they got there she was very ill and the doctor was unable to save her.

4. Tom and Ryan live with their mum and dad. They both have asthma and have to use an inhaler. Their parents both smoke in the house.

5. Lily and her brother David often get their own breakfast. They eat crisps and sweets. By the middle of the morning at school they find it hard to concentrate.

6. Tamandans has to walk to school; it is 3 miles away and takes her an hour. When she gets there she has a bowl of maize porridge. She has the same again when she gets home. She is small for her age.

7. A group of children in the P6 class often mess about and the teacher has to spend lots of time dealing with them.

8. Mercy and her mother walk to the river to fetch water for their family twice a day. Sometimes the family become sick as the water is not always clean.

9. Mark is 9 years old, and his mum insists on being in the same room as him when he is using the internet and checks what he is doing. Mark does not like this and they have many arguments.

10. The girls at St Mary's primary school are reluctant to go to school as they share the toilets with the boys and there are no locks on the doors.

Aims

- To be aware of the diversity of houses within Scotland and Malawi
- To find out about the similarities between homes in Scotland and Malawi
- To explore reasons why homes are different in Scotland and Malawi

What you need

- Photos of different types of houses in Malawi and Scotland
- Large sheets of flip chart paper / sugar paper
- Coloured sticky dots

What to do (1): (Levels 1 & 2)

Place a selection of photos showing different types of house in Scotland and Malawi around the classroom. Ask pupils to look at all the pictures and put a blue coloured dot on houses they think are in Scotland and a red coloured dot on houses which they think are in Malawi. Now ask the pupils to choose the house they would like to live in and stand next to it. Why did they choose this house? Pupils discuss reasons in groups and then feedback their choices to the class. Reveal to the class which countries the houses are in and group the pictures into houses in Malawi and houses in Scotland. Hold a plenary discussion using the teacher prompts points.

Teacher prompts

Which houses were not chosen? Why?
What made some more popular?
How did you decide if houses were in Scotland or Malawi?
Were you surprised about where some of the houses were?
What do you notice about the houses in Scotland? Are they all the same?
What do you notice about houses in Malawi? Are they all the same?
What is similar in all the photos of houses?
What are some of the differences?

What to do (2): (Level 2)

In groups, pupils are given a photo of a house in Malawi to stick into the middle of a large sheet of paper.

Each group nominates a scribe. Using a black pen, each group writes down all the things that their homes have in common with the home in Malawi. Using a red pen, the students write down all the things which are different. Discuss the similarities and differences.

As a class make a list of some of the reasons for differences: building materials, location, climate, family size, wealth / poverty, urban / rural. This list can be added to as they work through the topic. Pupils can then summarise their findings and create two lists: 1. 'Things homes in Scotland and Malawi have in common' (e.g. people live in homes, homes share common physical features, homes provide protection from the environment, people cook, sleep, relax and play in their homes). 2. 'Reasons for the variety of homes *within* Scotland and Malawi' (e.g. the number of people who live there, urban / rural, rich/ poor, old / modern, purpose of house e.g. farmhouse).
Assessment opportunity

Teacher prompts

Which similar activities might take place in the home sleeping / eating etc?
Are some of these activities done differently?
Do you think the people feel the same way about their homes as you do?
How do the people who live there help to make it a home?

Reflection and evaluation

Houses may look very different but each home is a special place for the people who live in it. There are a number of different reasons why homes are different, including, but not exclusively, wealth / poverty. There are lots of similarities and differences between houses within Scotland and house within Malawi.

Further ideas

Pupils choose a house in Malawi and imagine that they are going to visit the people who live there. They can write some questions they would like to ask them. Pupils can write a letter to the people in their chosen home, tell them about themselves and their families and ask about theirs.

Go to the CD ROM to find out which homes are in Scotland and Malawi.

HOMES

What is it like to live here?

Aims
- To engage empathetically with life in Malawi
- To produce a piece of descriptive writing or a word bank

What you need
- Photograph of a house in Malawi for each pupil
- Photograph of each pupil (or pupils can draw a small picture of themselves)
- Blu tac

What to do
Show the class a photograph of a house in Malawi. Ask the pupils to imagine that they are in the photo, and to think about what they can see, hear, smell and feel. Use the teacher prompts below. Elicit key words from pupils around each of the four senses and create a word bank.
Organise pupils in pairs and give each pair a photograph of a house in Malawi. Ask them to add a photo or drawing of themselves to the picture. Ask the pupils to imagine that they are in the photo and this is where they live.
Ask the pupils to again think about what they can see, hear, smell and feel using the word bank. Write their ideas next to the picture.

Pupils write an imaginative piece describing what it is like to be in their photo. **Assessment opportunity** Depending on the ability of the class you can start (or finish) the activity at different points.

Teacher prompts
What can you see? Who is with you? What time of day is it? Is it hot or cold?
What can you hear? Is it quiet? Is it noisy? Can you hear other people talking/laughing/singing/shouting? What is going on?
Can you smell anything? Is anyone cooking? Is anyone cleaning?
How do you feel? Are you happy/sad / tired / hungry?

Reflection and evaluation
Share the pupils' work. Can they match the descriptions with the pictures? Have they looked carefully at the picture? What evidence did they use to write their description?

Aims
- To explore pupils' perceptions of their own community
- To create a whole class map of the area where they live
- To agree on what is important for a community to thrive

What you need
- Large sheets of paper
- String, coloured pens, etc to create large class map

What to do
Discuss with the class how they and their families belong to a wider community and they are now going to look at this.

With the pupils, draw a map* of the school on a large sheet of paper.

Discuss the different areas, what they are used for and when the pupils visit them.

Put the map onto the wall. This will become the focus of the map of the local community the pupils will create.

Locate the pupils' homes around the school.

The pupils should now individually draw a map* of their route to school. These can then be added to the larger map.

Review what is on the map and elicit from the pupils other important things in their local community which are missing: shops, recreational areas, hospitals etc

Discuss with the pupils why these things are important and how they help the people in the community to have a good life.

You might also want to encourage the pupils to think about what things might improve their community.

Teacher prompts
What things are important in our community?

How do we use them? When do we use them?

Do all people in the community need these things?

Are there any other things which would make our life in our community better?

Reflection and evaluation
The pupils go on to compare their community with a community in Malawi in *Rights Activity 2: Our Community and Ernest's Community*

---

* The maps should reflect the pupil's perceptions of their school and their route to school and highlight things which are significant to them rather than focusing on accuracy.

Aims
- To find out about Ernest's community in Malawi and to compare it with their own
- To agree what is important for communities in Scotland and in Malawi
- To think about how communities support our rights

What you need
- The map which the class has created
- Enlarged copies of Ernest's map of his village
(*see opposite page*)

What to do
In pairs give pupils copies of Ernest's map. Read them the extract about Ernest's day and ask them to colour in, on his map, the places he talks about in his village. Organise the class so they can come up in pairs and compare Ernest's map with the class map.

They should note down what things are on both maps and what things are only in Ernest's village or on their map. Activity sheet *Our Community and Ernest's* on the CD ROM can be used to record their findings.

Discuss with the pupils which things are similar and which are different in the two communities.

Remind pupils of the work they have done on children's rights. Discuss ways in which the community can support children's rights: schools, hospital, leisure facilities, etc. Highlight or add them to Ernest's map and the class map.

Pupils can create a concentric circle diagram showing how they, their family and their community support their rights. **Assessment opportunity**

Diagram showing concentric circles

Me – eat healthy food, take exercise, listen to my teacher

My family – place to live, food, care

My community – health care, school, leisure facilities

Teacher prompts
What things can be found on both maps?
What things are on Ernest's map but not on yours?
Can you think why?
What things are on your map but not on Ernest's?
Can you think why?
How does the community support your rights and Ernest's rights?

Reflection and evaluation
Homes and families are part of a community. Communities and families have an important role to play in supporting children's rights.

Ernest's map of his village

NAMAKASU VILLAGE

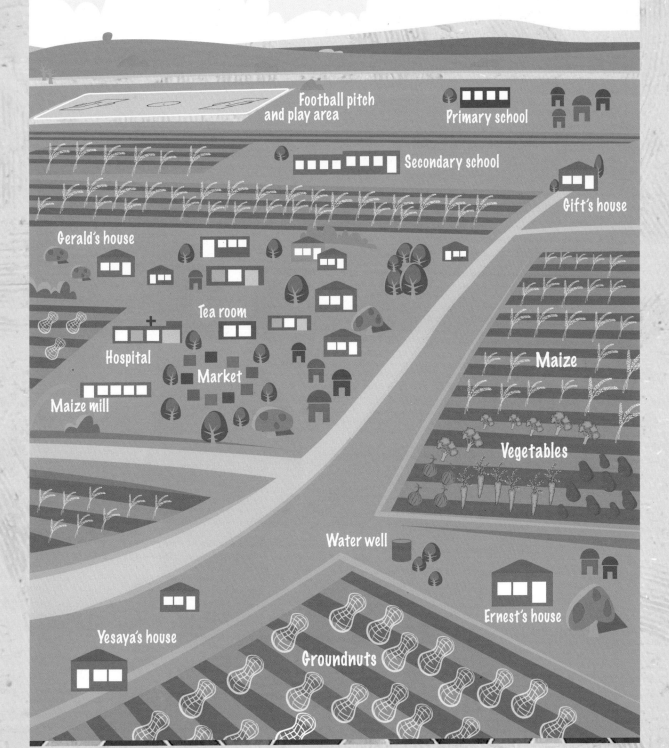

Football pitch and play area

Primary school

Secondary school

Gift's house

Gerald's house

Tea room

Hospital

Market

Maize mill

Maize

Vegetables

Water well

Ernest's house

Yesaya's house

Groundnuts

Aims

- To think about the games and toys young people play with
- To begin to consider the similarities and differences between play and toys in Scotland and in Malawi

What you need

- Photos of children playing in Malawi

What to do

Pupils sit in a circle on the floor.
Ask them about their favourite toys and what makes them special.
Ask them about the toys they play with, the games they play and where they play.
Put the photos of the children playing in Malawi on the floor in the middle of the circle.
Discuss what the children are doing, what they are playing with and where are they playing.
Talk about any games or toys that are similar to those the pupils play with.
Draw out similarities.
Ask the pupils to think about all the games they play that don't require toys. Record them on a flip chart or ask pupils to draw their own examples.
Group the games according to type: role play, imaginary games, team games, etc.
Pupils can add to the list as you continue with the topic.

Teacher prompts

What toys do you play with?
What are they made from?
What games do you play?
What toys are the children in Malawi playing with?
What games are the children in Malawi playing?
Do you always need toys to play games?
What games do you play that don't require toys or equipment?
What do you like about playing?
Do you think all children play?

Reflection and evaluation

All children play.
We don't need toys to be able to play.

Photo: Mairi MacDonald

Aims
- To begin to consider the similarities and differences between play and toys in Scotland and Malawi

What you need
- Photographs of children playing games in Malawi
- A big sheet of paper for each group
- A red, blue and black pen for each group.

What to do
Organise class into groups of 3 or 4.

Give each group a photo stuck on to a large piece of paper.

Ask the pupils to discuss what is happening in the picture. Encourage them to look closely at the images and look for clues in the photo. They can then note down with a blue pen what they can see and what is happening in the picture. Now ask the pupils to think about similarities between themselves and the child in the picture using the prompts below. They should write these around the photo using a red pen. Encourage them to focus on exploring the toys and play in the image.

Then ask them to think about what they think are some differences between themselves and the child in the photo and write it down using a black pen. Finally, ask them to think of two questions they would like to ask about their photo and write them at the bottom of the paper.

Each group can feed back to the rest of the class about what they have observed from their photo and what they wanted to know about it.

Display the photo work around the room and draw out key similarities and differences the pupils have found in the photos. Finding answers to the questions the students have posed could be a starting point for a subsequent lesson.

Teacher prompts
What are the children doing?
Where are the children playing?
Where do you play?
What are they playing with?
Do you have similar / the same toys?
What materials are the toys made from?
Do you play a similar / the same game?
Do you always need toys / equipment to play games?

Reflection and evaluation
Encourage the pupils to see that all children play, that their toys are often similar but made from different materials and that we don't always need toys to play.

Key similarities and differences can be recorded by the pupils and added to as they work through the topic.

TOYS

Aims
• Introduce pupils to the design process
• Make a football out of used materials

What you need
• Football clip (CD ROM)
• Plastic bags and newspapers (lots)
• String, strong wool, twine, elastic bands
• Scissors

What to do
Show the class the clip of the boys playing with the football they have made and discuss what would be important if they were to try and design a ball. With the whole class, discuss and devise a design brief such as 'make a ball that will be strong enough to last through a game of football'. Organise class into groups or pairs. Ask each group to brainstorm the task, deciding how they will set about it and what they need to consider. More able groups can write a design brief and a set of instructions for making the football. Make footballs and test them by playing football with them. They should then discuss how effective the methods were and any ideas for improving the design.

More able pupils can devise a method for testing their balls and make a grid to evaluate their results. They could then revisit their design instructions and think how they would change them and improve the design of their footballs.

Teacher prompts
It will need to be strong.
What if the ground is wet?
It will need to stay together.
It might need to be tight.
Should it be hard or soft?
Should it be big or small?
How many bags will we need?

Reflection and evaluation
Encourage pupils to reflect on what its like to make and build a toy rather than just use a bought one.

TOYS What happens to old toys?

Aims
- To think about issues of sustainability
- To investigate what happens to old toys

What to do
Discuss with the pupils occasions when they get new toys.
Discuss what happens to their old toys when they have finished with them.

Level 1: pupils could record what they do with their
old toys by making a class pictograph.
Brainstorm the various things which happen to the toys (bin, give to
younger friends/family members, charity shop, sell on eBay, etc.). The
pictograph could be added to by asking pupils in other classes as well.

Level 2: pupils could carry out a survey in the school
to investigate what happens to old toys.
Organise pupils into groups and ask them to brainstorm questions. Different
groups can survey different classes and present their findings in a number
of ways using different types of graphs/charts. **Assessment opportunity**
Hold a plenary discussion using the reflection and evaluation points below.
Pupils may want to run a campaign using posters and assemblies
to encourage pupils in the school to recycle or pass on old
toys. They could measure the impact their campaign has had
by carrying out their survey again. **Enterprise Activity**

Teacher prompts
What happens to old toys? (Recycle them, pass on to family and
friends, throw them away, give them to a charity shop)
How do we decide what we do with them?

Reflection and evaluation
What happens to most old toys?
Is it better to reuse old toys or throw them away? Why?
*Children in Malawi often make and play with toys made
from recycled materials. Encourage the pupils to see
the positive aspects of this, in comparison to our
'throw away' society, rather than simply thinking
'they don't get new toys because they are poor.'
Some benefits are: sustainable use of materials,
developing skills in designing and building toys,
increases the value of the toy, etc.*

Further ideas
Pupils could set up and hold a toy
exchange at school. **Enterprise Activity**

TOYS

Aims

- To develop awareness of how creating a set of rules in advance can avoid conflict
- To encourage co-operative play amongst children

What you need

- PowerPoint *Games in Malawi* (CD ROM)

What to do

Show the pupils the PowerPoint and have a discussion about the games the children in Malawi are playing in the pictures. What equipment is being used? Do we play similar games / have similar toys? Discuss with the pupils the idea that we have rules for 'happy play'. Organise the pupils into groups and ask them to brainstorm all the things they need for happy play. Then ask them to make a list of the rules needed for happy play: take turns, include everyone, etc. Feedback and make a class list of 'Rules for Happy Play'. Have a class discussion about rules.

Teacher prompts

What do we need for happy play? (safe environment, friends, etc.) Who makes the rules when they play? Why do we have rules? Who enforces the rules? Does everyone keep the rules? What happens if someone breaks the rules? What do you do if someone else breaks the rules?

Reflection and evaluation

Are games important? What do we learn from them? Why do we play them? Are they the same for all children?

Further ideas

Draw a map of your playground and map out what is played where. Design a playground where there is space for everyone to play.

Photo: Gavin Parks

FOOD & FARMING

What do you know about farming? (Level 2)

Aims

• To assess knowledge and understanding of farming in Scotland and Malawi

What you need

• A copy of activity sheet *Food and Farming* – True or False per pair

What to do

Explain to the class that they are going to place themselves on an 'agree / disagree' line (CD ROM) in response to the statements you read out about farming in Scotland. After reading each statement, give pupils time to decide how much they agree or disagree and place themselves on the line. Ask for volunteers to explain their position.

Statement 1: Most of the food we eat is produced in the UK.
Statement 2: Most of the food we eat is grown or raised on farms.
Statement 3: In Scotland we could do without farms if we had to.

In pairs, pupils complete the true / false chart on the activity sheet. They should discuss and agree on each answer. Encourage them to draw from their knowledge and perceptions of farms.
Put each pair together with another pair to discuss their answers. They can make changes to their original answers as a result of their discussion if they wish.
Hold a plenary discussion to reflect on pupils' responses.

Assessment opportunity: This is a recorded baseline activity which can be redone at the end of the topic to see if the pupils' thinking has changed.

Teacher prompts

Read the statements carefully.
Discuss with your partner if you think they are true, false or don't know. Think about whether the statements are the same for all farms in Scotland and Malawi.

Reflection and evaluation

What did they think for each of the statements?
Did they agree? Why or why not?
How do your responses differ for Scotland and Malawi?
Where do your ideas about farming in Malawi come from?
Challenge any misconceptions and stereotypical ideas around farming.

Agree ═══════════════════ Disagree

FOOD & FARMING

Aims

- To consider the key things we look for when choosing our food

What you need

- Activity sheet *What do we want from our food?* Cut up for each group (Level 1 and Level 2 cards available to select as appropriate – Level 1 cards on CD ROM).

What to do

Organise pupils into groups and ask them to brainstorm what things we need to think about when buying food.

Level 1: Pupils discuss the reasons for choosing what food to buy as suggested on the cards. Ask them if they want to add in any of their own ideas. In groups, they can select the 2 or 3 most important things to think about when buying food.

Level 2: Give each group a set of cards and ask them to 'diamond rank' (see diagram) the cards in order of importance.

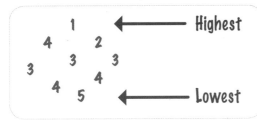

Share group decisions with the class. Ask the pupils if there are any other things to consider when buying food. Can the whole class reach a consensus about 2 or 3 things that mattered most when choosing our food?

Teacher prompts

Why do you think these are important?
Do you agree or disagree with it being important when choosing what food to buy?
Can you explain why?
Can you agree as a group where to place the cards?
If there is disagreement in a group, maybe they can take a vote.

Reflection and evaluation

Do all the groups agree on what is most important when choosing our food?
What did you find easy or difficult to agree on?
Are there other matters we should take into consideration when choosing our food?

Further ideas

Assessment opportunity: Explore the issues the class thought to be most important using a development compass rose. (CD ROM)

Activity sheet – What do we want from our food? (Level 2)

LOCALLY PRODUCED	ETHICAL	FRESH
KIND TO ANIMALS	GOOD FOR WILDLIFE	PRICE
HEALTHY FOR US	FAIRLY TRADED	GOOD QUALITY

Adapted from TIDE, Food and Farming – local and global

Aims

- To understand the difference between cash crops and subsistence farming
- To begin to explore some of the issues around subsistence farming in Malawi

What you need

- Sets of *What have I got?* and *What do I do?* cards cut up for each group

What to do

Ask the class if most people in Scotland live in the countryside or in cities and towns.

Explain that, in Malawi, 90% of the population live in rural areas and most people have some land and grow food on it.

Organise the class into groups and give them a set of *What have I got?* and *What do I do?* cards. The pupils should match the cards with the statements.

Feedback the answers and elicit from the students that some farmers are growing crops to sell (cash crops) and that some are growing food for themselves (subsistence farming).

Ask the pupils to decide which farms are in Scotland and which are in Malawi.

Discuss the pupils' choices.

Explain that most people in Malawi grow maize and some vegetables for the family to eat. Some people may grow cash crops such as sugar cane and tobacco. In Scotland, most farming is for cash crops though some people still grow fruit and vegetables for themselves.

Pupils can create their own definitions for 'cash crops' and 'subsistence farming' and add these to their word bank started in *Topic Activity 4: Farming Vocabulary* (CD ROM).

Assessment opportunity: In groups, pupils can work together to produce a poster which shows the key differences between 'cash crops' and 'subsistence farming'.

Teacher prompts

Will the people eat the produce they grow?

Will the people sell the produce they grow?

Do they grow a variety of things?

What will happen if the crops don't grow properly?

Do you think the consequences are the same for here and in Malawi? Why?

Reflection and evaluation

Subsistence farming in Malawi is explored in more detail in *Topic Activity 7: Subsistence Farming in Malawi*

Information for teachers

Farm 1 and Farmer A (Scotland)

Farm 2 and Farmer B (Scotland)

Farm 3 and Farmer C (Malawi)

Farm 4 and Farmer D (Scotland)

Farm 5 and Farmer E (Malawi)

Farm 6 and Farmer F (Malawi)

FOOD & FARMING

What have I got?

FARM 1
This is a medium sized plot of land. Much of it is steep and rocky. There is some steep pastureland and a small area of flat, fertile land. I live here with my wife and three children.

FARM 2
This is a very large farm with lots of very flat and fertile land. I am single and live in a nearby town.

FARM 3
This is a small rural village where I live with my wife, five children and my parents. We have a large field and a small fertile plot. There is also some common grazing land which all the village can use.

FARM 4
This is a small, flat and fertile piece of land close to a large town. It used to be much bigger but land was used for a new road, a large supermarket and extra housing.

FARM 5
This is a large farm with flat fertile land. I live here with my family and farm workers.

FARM 6
This is a medium size farm in a rural area with flat, fertile land. I live here with my family.

What do I do?

FARMER A
I keep a milking cow and some sheep on the pastureland. I grow some vegetables on the fertile land to feed my family. I am going to convert the old barn into a house to rent. My wife has a job as a teacher.

FARMER B
I grow wheat which I sell to a large bakery. I employ around 15 people and have invested in tractors and harvesting equipment.

FARMER C
I grow maize in the large field and I will grow vegetables like sweet potatoes, pumpkins, tomatoes and greens in the small plot. My wife has a job as a teacher.

FARMER D
I grow a wide variety of vegetables and soft fruit. I employ a large number of people at harvesting time as most of the work needs to be done by hand and is very seasonal. I sell my produce at the local farmers' market, supply soft fruit to local restaurants and shops in summer and run a vegetable box delivery scheme.

FARMER E
I grow sugar cane which is processed on the farm and then sold to a large company. I employ a large number of people to work the land who live in the accommodation block next to our house.

FARMER F
I grow sugar cane to sell through the local co-operative set up with my neighbours. We have managed to secure a contract with a fair trade organisation. I also grow some maize and a variety of vegetables.

Aims

- To explore some of the issues faced by subsistence farmers in Malawi
- To create an 'issues tree' (CD ROM) around subsistence farming in Malawi

What you need

- Copies of pupil information sheet *Subsistence farming in Malawi*
- Teacher information sheet *Subsistence farming in Malawi* (CD ROM)

What to do

In pairs, pupils read the pupil information sheet on subsistence farming.

Ask the pupils to highlight or underline the problems that the farmers in the countryside in Malawi have.

Explain that you are going to create an 'issues tree' to explore some of these problems. See diagram opposite.

Draw a large tree on the board or chart paper. In the trunk write 'subsistence farming in Malawi'. Elicit from the pupils the problems they have found for subsistence farmers. Write these effects on the branches.

Now fill in the roots with the reasons for subsistence farming.

Finally encourage the pupils to find solutions to some of the problems (the branches) and write them in the leaves.

Teacher prompts

Does the work on the land take a long time? Why? What could improve this?

Does the land always get enough water? How could this be improved?

Do the farmers have cash to buy food? Why? How could they earn money?

Who owns the land?

Is there enough land to feed a family?

What happens when the family gets bigger?

Why do children sometimes not go to school?

Reflection and evaluation

The majority of the population in Malawi are subsistence farmers and they face many problems.

Climate change is having a big impact on farming in Malawi. Climate change is looked at in more detail in the Water topic.

Often fertile land is taken for cash crops such as tobacco and sugar rather than for food.

Pupil information sheet

Most people in Malawi live in the countryside (rural areas). Most people living in the countryside are farmers and grow food for themselves and their families to live on. They are called subsistence farmers. The farmers grow maize which they will store and keep to eat. They also have small vegetable gardens where they will grow things such as potatoes, tomatoes, pumpkins and greens. Sometimes, if they have any spare maize or vegetables they can sell them at the market to make some money.

Most of the work on the land is done by hand. The women in village usually look after the vegetable gardens while the men look after the maize crops. This is very time consuming and sometimes the children have to stay home from school to help with the farm.

People are given their land by the village leaders. This means they do not own the land and might not want to spend money improving it. As a family grows in size, the land is split into smaller areas so everyone can grow their own food. This can make it difficult to produce enough food.

In Malawi it rains from November to April. This is when the maize is grown. It is planted when the rains start and harvested in March and April.

The crops need rain in order to grow. If the crops don't grow then the farmer and his family will not have enough food to eat and they will be hungry. Sometimes the rain does not come and there is a drought. Sometimes there is too much rain and there is a flood. Drought and flood can stop the food from growing.

The farmers in Malawi have found that the rain is often not coming when they think it will so it makes it hard for them to plant and grow their crops. This is because of climate change.

Issues tree

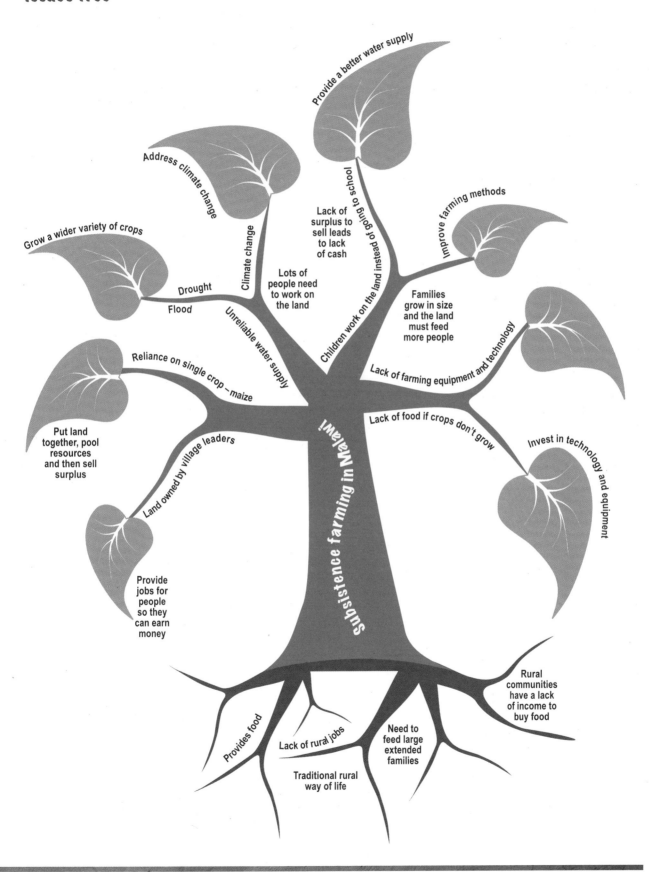

- Provide a better water supply
- Address climate change
- Grow a wider variety of crops
- Climate change
- Drought
- Flood
- Lack of surplus to sell leads to lack of cash
- Lots of people need to work on the land
- Children work on the land instead of going to school
- Improve farming methods
- Families grow in size and the land must feed more people
- Unreliable water supply
- Reliance on single crop – maize
- Lack of farming equipment and technology
- Put land together, pool resources and then sell surplus
- Land owned by village leaders
- Lack of food if crops don't grow
- Invest in technology and equipment
- Provide jobs for people so they can earn money
- Subsistence farming in Malawi
- Rural communities have a lack of income to buy food
- Provides food
- Lack of rural jobs
- Need to feed large extended families
- Traditional rural way of life

WATER **Fair use of water (Level 2)**

Aims
• To encourage group discussion and debate
• To understand that access to clean water is a right for all

What you need
• Sets of activity sheet *Fair Use of Water*, cut up for each group

What to do
Divide class into groups and give each one a set of water statement cards.
Ask each group to make three columns: agree, disagree and not sure.
Ask pupils to discuss each statement and place the cards in one column.
Ask each group to share with the whole class the statements they
have in the 'disagree' column and the 'not sure' column.

Teacher prompts
Sometimes there are no 'right answers', just opinions.
What evidence is there for your answer / opinion?
Can you agree as a group?

Reflection and evaluation
Did the pupils mostly agree with their decisions of where to put
the statements? Which statements caused most debate? Why?
Is there much variation in the class?
Do pupils think that access to clean water is a right?
Do we all have the same access to clean water around the world?

Assessment opportunity: It would be useful to repeat this
exercise after pupils have completed the topic to see
how their attitudes to water have changed.

7. We need clean water
to be healthy.

1. We have plenty of water
in Scotland so there is no
need for us to use less water.

4. People in Scotland
waste water.

8. The amount of water
there is to drink depends
on how much rain falls.

2. Some countries will
never have enough water.

5. Lots of water is needed to
manufacture goods and food.

9. Families need water
for many different
domestic jobs.

3. We can't help countries
where their people don't
have clean water.

6. Farmers need to have
water to grow good crops.

10. People should be
able to use as much
water as they want.

Water and the Daily Routine

WATER

Aims

- To think about our everyday uses of water
- To recognise the common uses of water over the world
- To compare water usage in Scotland and Malawi

What you need

- *A Day in the Life of Molisha* (see next page)
- Activity sheet, *Water usage in Malawi and Scotland* for each pupil

What to do

In groups, ask pupils to brainstorm all the ways they use water in their homes.
Suggest that they think through a day from the time when they get up to when they go to bed.
Pupils fill in the first part of activity sheet about water use in their home in Scotland
Read *A Day in the life of Molisha* to the class.
Ask pupils to put up their hand every time they think that Molisha is using water.
Ask them to complete the second part of the activity sheet for water use in Molisha's home.
Ask class to suggest any other uses of water in homes in Malawi or Scotland.
Compare their use of water and Molisha's using the reflection and evaluation points.

Teacher prompts

Uses of water: drinking (tea, coffee, juice) cleaning teeth, washing, showering, having a bath, flushing the toilet, watering house plants watering the garden, washing a car, cleaning windows, washing clothes in a washing machine, washing vegetables, cooking.

Reflection and evaluation

Discuss similarities and differences in uses of water
Where does water come from for our daily activities? Where does Molisha's water come from?
What are similarities and differences between their lives and Molisha's life?

Further ideas

What else is water useful for in our lives?
Could include: farmers watering fields (irrigation systems); factories (food production, clothes dyeing industry); hydro-electric power; transport (ferry); fishing; recreational uses of water (sailing, canoeing, kayaking, surfing, swimming, etc.).

Activity Sheet: Water usage in Malawi and Scotland

Water usage in Molisha's home (Malawi)		Water usage in my home (Scotland)	
Time of day	What the family used water for	Time of day	What my family used water for
Morning and Breakfast		Morning and Breakfast	
Lunchtime		Lunchtime	
Afternoon		Afternoon	
Evening/ night time		Evening/ night time	
Where does the water used by the family come from?	All the water is drawn (lifted) from a well in buckets by Molisha and her mother	Where does the water used by the family come from?	From taps in the house in the bathroom and kitchen

1.

My name is Molisha Katsekera and I am 14 years old. I live in the village of Namakasu in Malawi.

2. *Namakasu has a weekly market, small hospital, school and a maize mill. People go to the maize mill for their maize to be made into flour to make our staple food which is called nsima.*

3. *I live with my father and mother, my 16 year old sister Ether and my 10 year old brother Ernest. My older brothers, Aubrey and Wilfred, stay in the village and usually eat the evening meal with us.*

4. *My father is a businessman who has a tea room beside the market which he runs with my brother Aubrey who is 21. He sells tea, nsima and scones (small bread loaves) at the tea room.*

5. *My mother cooks our nsima and draws water. With my brothers, Aubrey and Wilfred, she digs the land which we farm where we grow maize and groundnuts.*

6. *I get up at six o'clock when the sun rises and my sister and I sweep the compound. It takes about fifteen minutes. Then I wash the plates from the meal the night before. We wash them in the morning because it is too dark to wash them after the meal. Then I draw two buckets of water for washing from the well and take a bath (wash).*

7.

For breakfast I have tea with four dessert spoons of sugar and maize porridge. At twenty past seven I walk to the primary school.

Each day at school starts with assembly. We sing the national anthem every day. **8.** Then lessons start. I am in the last year of primary school. My class is standard eight and there are 36 pupils in my class.

I usually sit next to Karden and Crystal. My favourite lessons are English and Social Studies. At break-time **9.** I usually play 'Fly' with my friends. We use a ball made from recycled plastic bags to play 'Fly', just like the ones the boys play football with.

10.

I come home for lunch at one o'clock. We eat nsima and turnips.

11.

It is important to pass the exams at the end of primary school. I want to pass them so I can go to secondary school. My older brothers have completed the four years of secondary school and my sister Ether is in Form Two. So in the afternoon I walk from my house and go back to school and work with my class until four o'clock.

12.

Then I go home and wash the plates from lunch and play with my friends. After that I help my mother and sister to cook the evening meal and we eat nsima all together just after the sun has set a six o'clock.

13.

At half past six I go back to school until twenty past eight. We use paraffin lamps to read in the dark. Then I go home and Esther and I go to the bedroom we share to sleep on the mat.

WATER

Water usage in Malawi

Aims

- To calculate how you would use 15 litres of water per day
- To raise awareness of the importance of vital resources such as water and our responsibility to use them sustainably

What you need

- Water activity sheet *Water Use Guide for Homes in Scotland* for each group (CD ROM)

What to do

This activity works best once the pupils have done Activity 3 *Recording Water Usage* (CD ROM). Recap the daily uses of water and the amount of water used for these tasks. Organise pupils into groups and tell them that on average a person in rural Malawi uses 5 buckets (15 litres) of water per day. Give groups the *Water Use Guide*. In their groups they must decide how they would use their 15 litres of water. They should create a pie chart to show how they would use their 15 litres of water. Whole class feedback and discussion Pupils could go on to think about how they could conserve water at school. See Further ideas.

Teacher prompts

Which are the most important or essential uses of water? Which activities could you still do but with less water? Could you use some water for more than one activity? Which activities could you not do at all?

Reflection and evaluation

Many people in Malawi have to carefully plan and prioritise their daily use of water. Cooking and drinking have to be the most important tasks for water usage. A lack of water can mean a risk to health as there is less water for personal washing, clothes washing, drainage and sanitation.

Further ideas

This activity highlights how people in Malawi are forced to conserve and think carefully about their water usage. Ask the pupils to think about ways of saving water in their school or at home and carry out an investigation into how to conserve water. This could lead to an awareness campaign throughout the school. Enterprise activity

The comparison sheet can be used for a number of maths activities depending on the ability and level of the pupils.

WATER

Aims

- To understand the consequences if our water supply is cut off
- To consider the consequences of not having a water supply in Malawi

What you need

- Large piece of flip chart paper for each group.
- Several large marker pens
- Blank consequences chain drawn on board
- Copies of Molisha's *A Day in the Life* for each group (see pages 32 & 33)

What to do

Explain that water is a finite resource that we take for granted in this country because it is so easy to turn on the tap. But we are going to imagine what might happen if we were not able to get water from the tap in our houses. Ask pupils if they have ever been in a situation where they had no water in the house. If so what were the reasons for this? Brainstorm other reasons why this might happen. (Local water mains repairs, damaged local water supply, burst tank or house water pipes) Explain that they are going to use a consequences chain to think about what would happen if the water is cut off. Write 'water shut off' in the issue circle. Discuss some of the problems they would have. They then need to follow the chain to think of the consequences of each. See example below. Divide class into groups and ask them to discuss and complete a chain. Each group should share their ideas of the consequences of no water. Discuss some of the issues which arise. Repeat the consequences chain for Molisha's family. What are some of the issues that arise for her family? Compare the consequences chains and hold a plenary discussion using the reflection points below.

Teacher prompts

What jobs would not be done?
What would happen if you couldn't wash dishes, wash yourself, etc?

Reflection and evaluation

Would the consequences of not having water be the same or different for Molisha's family? If there are differences what would they be and why?
Clean water is essential for health and hygiene but many people in the world do not have access to clean water or enough water.
Access to clean water is an important right.

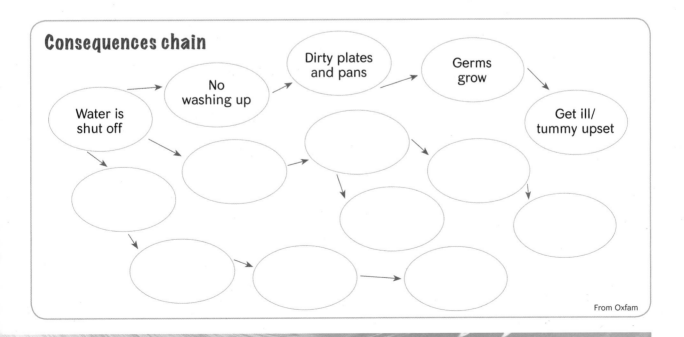

Consequences chain

Water is shut off → No washing up → Dirty plates and pans → Germs grow → Get ill/ tummy upset

From Oxfam

Acknowledgments

Written by Charlotte Dwyer with contributions from Susan McIntosh,
Della Rae, Ruth Tibbs, Susan Arnott and Margaret Wynd.

With special thanks to Diana Ellis, Mairi MacDonald,
Richard Ward, Isabel Ross, Humphrey Savieri and Doreen Chanje.

Photos reproduced with kind permission from Susan Arnott,
Roger Bamfield, Liz Drawbell, Kate Dresser, Diana Ellis,
Marianned Farish, Maggie Lunan, Sheena MacGillivray,
Gavin Parks, Christopher Ross, Humphrey Savieri,
Scotland Malawi Partnership, Ruth Tibbs, Tradecraft and Wateraid.
Front cover main image © Audioslave #3610065

We are very grateful to Ernest, Molisha and their family for allowing
us to use their photos and for sharing their day in the life stories.

Design by www.contextdesigns.co.uk
CD ROM development by www.eskimoonline.com

Funded by The Scottish Government with support from the Global Learning Project (DFID)

The Scottish Government